MW01093524

https://campsite.bio/unitedlibrary

Table of Contents

Disclaimer

This biography book is a work of nonfiction based on the public life of a famous person. The author has used publicly available information to create this work. While the author has thoroughly researched the subject and attempted to depict it accurately, it is not meant to be an exhaustive study of the subject. The views expressed in this book are those of the author alone and do not necessarily reflect those of any organization associated with the subject. This book should not be taken as an endorsement, legal advice, or any other form of professional advice. This book was written for entertainment purposes only.

Introduction

Marilyn Monroe's readers are invited to delve into the captivating and tumultuous life of Norma Jeane Mortenson, the American actress, model, and singer who transcended the silver screen to become an enduring symbol of glamour, sensuality, and the changing times of the 1950s and early 1960s.

Born and raised in Los Angeles under challenging circumstances, Marilyn Monroe's journey from a troubled childhood in foster homes to becoming a Hollywood legend is a testament to her resilience and determination. The book navigates her early years, from a teenage marriage to her serendipitous entry into the world of pin-up modeling and film contracts with major studios.

Monroe's meteoric rise to stardom is vividly portrayed, with a focus on her transformation into the quintessential "blonde bombshell". Her iconic roles in films like "Gentlemen Prefer Blondes" and "How to Marry a Millionaire" solidified her status as a cinematic treasure, while her personal life and image management added layers of complexity to her public persona.

The book explores Monroe's influence on popular culture, her strategic image management, and her pioneering efforts in founding her own film production company. It delves into her dedication to method acting and her critically acclaimed performances in films like "Bus Stop" and "Some Like It Hot."

However, Monroe's life was far from perfect, marked by addiction, mood disorders, and high-profile marriages. Her tragic death at the age of 36 shocked the world, leaving behind a legacy that continues to captivate audiences and inspire artists to this day.

"This book offers an intimate glimpse into the woman behind the legend, celebrating her extraordinary talent, beauty, and the enduring allure that makes her an icon of Hollywood's Golden Age.

Marilyn Monroe

Marilyn Monroe ([ˈmɛəɹɪlɪn mənˈɹoʊ]) was an American actress, model and singer, born on June 1ᵉʳ 1926 in Los Angeles and died on August 4 1962 in the same city.

She initially set her sights on modeling before being spotted by Ben Lyon and signing her first acting contract with 20th Century Fox in August 1946. By the early 1950s, she had become a Hollywood star and sex symbol. Her major film successes included *Les hommes préfèrent les blondes* (1953), *Sept Ans de réflexion* (1955) and *Certains l'aiment chaud* (1959), for which she won the Golden Globe for Best Actress in a Comedy in 1960.

Despite her great fame, her career left her unfulfilled, and her private life was unstable and fraught with uncertainty. She had failed marriages to baseball star Joe DiMaggio and writer Arthur Miller. Her role has since been played by leading actresses of subsequent generations: Isabelle Adjani, Emmanuelle Seigner, Maggie Civantos, Michelle Williams and Ana de Armas.

Biography

Ancestry

Marilyn Monroe's great-great-grandparents were George Willis Hogan, born in 1823 in Kentucky (son of Zachariah Hogan and Delilah Marksberry), and Sarah Ann Owen, born in 1823 in Virginia (daughter of Edward Owen). They married on March 11, 1843. They have a son, Tilford Marion Hogan, and a daughter, Mary Ann (1844-1930).

Marilyn's great-grandparents were Tilford Marion Hogan (1851-1933) and Charlotte Virginia (Jennie) Nance (1857-?). They married in 1870 and lived in Missouri. They have four children, including Della, the second born. The other three children are Dora, Myrtle and William Marion.

Della (1876-1927, daughter of Tilford and Jennie) married Otis Elmer Monroe, a house painter ten years her senior, in 1899. They left for Mexico to work for a railroad company where she had been promised a good salary, then returned to California in 1903 for a better job with the Pacific Electric Railway. In 1902, while they were still in Mexico, Gladys (Marilyn's mother) was born. In 1905, the family had another child, Marion (1905-?).

Between 1903 and 1909, the family moved a dozen times, leading a precarious and unstable life. From 1907 onwards, Otis's health deteriorated. Hospitalized in 1908, he died in 1909 of neurological syphilis (progressive general paralysis), contracted as a result of the deplorable hygienic conditions he had experienced in Mexico, where the disease was epidemic. He is buried in Whittier. Della remarries twice, then divorces. She suffers from health problems. Her son Marion married a schoolmate. Della died of heart failure on August 23, 1927.

Marilyn's mother, Gladys Pearl Baker Mortensen Monroe (May 27, 1902 - March 11, 1984), born in Mexico of American parents, worked as an editor at Consolidated Film Industries (en).

On May 17, 1917, she married John Newton "Jasper" Baker, whose surname Marilyn adopted in 1938. The couple have two children: Robert Kermit "Jack" (born January 24, 1918) and Berniece Inez Gladys Baker Miracle (born July 30, 1919). On June 20, 1921, she filed for divorce on grounds of "cruelty and mental cruelty", but was accused in return of "indecent behavior and lust". The divorce was finalized on May 11, 1923. Gladys obtained custody of her children but, unable to care for them, she was forced to leave them with their father, who had moved to Kentucky and remarried. Robert died on August 16, 1933 at the age of 15. As for Berniece, she was not reunited with her mother until 1939, when she was committed to Agnews State Hospital for schizophrenia; it was then that she learned of the existence of her half-sister, Norma Jeane. Marilyn never knew her half-brother Hermitt Jack; on the other hand, she met her half-sister Berniece for the first time in 1944 in Tennessee.

Gladys had as many one-night stands as she did psychological and health problems, so Marilyn never knew the identity of her real father. Martin Edward Mortensen, born in 1897 and died in 1981, is the official father noted on Marilyn Monroe's birth certificate. He married Gladys on October 11, 1924; the couple separated in August 1925.

Childhood and adolescence

Marilyn Monroe was born on June 1er 1926 at Los Angeles General Hospital in California, under the name **Norma Jeane Mortenson** (instead of Mortensen, the registrar having made a spelling error)"" . She was, however, baptized as **Norma Jeane Baker**. While some sources claim that the name Norma Jeane came from Gladys's admiration for actresses Norma Talmadge and Jean Harlow, her sister, Berniece Baker Miracle, writes in her biography of Marilyn that her mother was inspired by the name of a friend's daughter, Norma Jean Cohen Seidman. She added an "e" to Jean, as was customary in California. However, Marilyn preferred to spell it "Norma Jean".

On the birth certificate appear the names of her mother, Gladys Monroe, and her husband at the time, Martin Edward Mortensen (1897-1981)′ , a Californian of Norwegian origin working as a gas meter reader. The couple had married on October 11, 1924, but separated in May 1925 (a year before Marilyn's birth); Mortensen obtained a divorce on August 15, 1928, for "abandonment of domicile".

Although she is a legitimate child′ , Marilyn has denied all her life that Mortensen is her father. When she was a child, her mother allegedly showed her a photograph of the man who was supposed to have been her father. She remembers him as having a thin moustache and a certain resemblance to Clark Gable′ . Following a lengthy investigation by French documentary filmmaker François Pomès, the mystery of Marilyn Monroe's biological father was solved. In 2021, DNA sequencing of samples of the star's hair taken at her autopsy and a saliva sample proved that she was the biological daughter of Charles Stanley Gifford (1898-1965), foreman at Consolidated Films Industries, which several biographers had been postulating for years″ . While in the process of divorce, Gladys had affairs with several men, including Gifford, her superior at Consolidated, and became pregnant. Gifford was married, but refused to recognize the child. Marilyn was therefore registered under the name of her mother's official husband at the time, Edward Mortensen. Stanley

Gifford refused to acknowledge any connection with Marilyn or Gladys until his death.

For a very long time, Gladys, regularly institutionalized because of her schizophrenic disorders with paranoid delusions, was unable to look after her daughter, who was placed in a foster home' and then in an orphanage. In the early days of her growing fame, Marilyn pretended that her mother had died, rather than admit that she was living in a psychiatric institution. She also exaggerated for a long time about her childhood, adding or removing certain facts to win public sympathy.

For the first seven years of her life, Norma Jeane was entrusted to Albert and Ida Bolender, neighbors of her grandmother Della, in Hawthorne, California. In her autobiography, Marilyn mentions that she didn't know who "this redheaded lady" (her mother) was, who visited her from time to time during this period. In 1933, she was able to live for a while with Gladys, who rented a room from the Atkinsons on Arbol Street (Hollywood), but she was committed the following year following another hysterical attack. In 1935, Grace McKee, Gladys' roommate, co-worker and best friend, asked to become Marilyn's guardian, which was formalized on March 27, 1936.

She attended Van Nuys High School in Los Angeles. In late 1940, Marilyn met Eleanor "Bebe" Goddard, daughter of

Grace McKee's husband, Doc Goddard. Long after the actress's death, Eleanor told a Marilyn exhibition that many of Monroe's anecdotes about the hardships of childhood - the whippings, the child servant, the hunger and the multiple foster homes [ref. needed] - had in fact been borrowed by the star from Goddard's early experiences. Nevertheless, she didn't hold it against him. After her father and Grace McKee left for West Virginia, Bebe continued to send him letters.

In 1941, Norma Jeane met James "Jim" Dougherty, a neighbor five years her senior and a worker in a Lockheed factory set up by actor Reginald Denny. Grace arranged the wedding, which took place on June 19, 1942, a few days after her sixteenth birthday. A year later, after dropping out of school, Jim joins the Merchant Navy, then in 1944 a B-17 crew over Germany, before returning to civilian life in the LAPD. Norma Jeane works on fireproofing aircraft and drone wings and inspecting parachutes for the Radioplane Company (en). It was in this factory that she was spotted by military photographers.

In 1944, she first met her half-sister, Bernice Baker Miracle, in Tennessee, her half-brother Hermitt Jack having already died. Her first quasi-professional photo is taken on June 26, 1945 by David Conover (en), US Army photographer for *Yank* magazine, as part of a US Army campaign to illustrate women's involvement in the war effort. She appears under the pseudonym "Norma Jeane Dougherty".

Modeling career

In 1946, she met Hungarian-born photographer Andre de Dienes (en), who took many portraits of her, including some nudes.

In May 1948, Marilyn Monroe posed nude for Tom Kelley in a wall calendar (known as the *Golden Dreams* calendar). In 1952, at a time when she was already well known, she fell victim to a blackmailer who threatened to expose her. Finally, Marilyn Monroe announced it herself, claiming financial need. In December 1953, some of these photos appeared in the first issue of *Playboy* magazine, her publisher Hugh Hefner having bought them back for $500. This bold move, which enabled the magazine's production to continue, was responsible for its growing success over the next two decades.

Within a few months, she was on the cover of some thirty *pin-up* magazines and began to make a name for herself as the "*Mmmmm girl*". In August 1945, she joined the Blue Book Modeling Agency headed by Emmeline Snively (it), where she took modeling classes at the in-house *Blue Book Models School* in Los Angeles. In December 1945, she shot her first test film for the agency, promoting swimwear. In February 1946, she lightened her hair color for a shampoo advertising campaign on the advice of Emmeline Snively (who reportedly told her: "Listen, darling, if you intend to succeed at this agency, you'll have to bleach and straighten your hair; your face is a little too round and a hair job will lengthen it").

First steps in cinema

Dreaming of becoming a film actress, she took acting lessons and continued to dye her hair light blond. With 33 magazine appearances to her credit and a desire to try out her hair, Norma Jeane attracts the attention of 20th Century Fox executive Ben Lyon, who arranges a screen test for her. Impressed by her blond hair, he reportedly declared: "This is the new Jean Harlow. She signed her first six-month contract with Fox on July 26, 1946, at a salary of $75 a week. On Ben Lyon's advice, she agreed to change her name to "Marilyn Monroe", the first name Marilyn being inspired by the actress Marilyn Miller and the name Monroe coming from her mother (she officially adopted this surname on February 23, 1956(en) Chris Bodenner, "The Day Norma Jean Died", on The Atlantic, February 24, 2016). It was again on the latter's recommendation that she divorced Jim, with whom she had little contact due to their estrangement, on October 2, 1946, Fox not believing in the future of a future star if she was already married.

Her career not taking off, she did promotional work as a model, and as such was elected "Honorary Queen" of the Castroville Artichoke Festival in 1948.

She made her first screen appearance in 1947 in *Bagarre pour une blonde* and *Dangerous Years*. In 1948, she signed a new six-month contract with Columbia, starring in the low-budget musical *Les Reines du music-hall*. The film was a flop, and her contract was not renewed. However, her appearance in the Marx Brothers' *Treasure Fishing* impressed the producers, who sent her to New York to promote the film.

During a photo shoot at the Racquet Club of Palm Springs (en), she attracts the attention of Johnny Hyde, vice-president of the William Morris Agency, who agrees to become her artistic agent and signs her to a 3-year contract on March 2, 1950, becoming, according to some rumors, her lover. He helped her create her star image; he took her to a facialist and even paid for her to have a rhinoplasty and genioplasty at the famous Beverly Hills surgeon Michael Gurdin. He then landed her a role in John Huston's *When the City Sleeps.* Critics praised the quality of her performance.

Refusing to depend on Johnny Hyde, who was in love with her, and lacking the money, she posed nude under the pseudonym "Mana Monroe" for the photographer Tom Kelley (en), in calendar photos that would tour the world a few years later when she became famous (see Nudity in her career).

Noticed by Joseph L. Mankiewicz, who saw in her a "great talent", she was cast by him in *Eve* (1950) alongside Bette Davis. Given the success of her latest films, Marilyn negotiates a seven-year contract with 20th Century Fox in December 1950. In September, *Photoplay Magazine* publishes the first feature article on her: "*How a star is born*", referring to William A. Wellman's *A Star Is Born* (1937), and awards her the Rising Star award.

The following year, she enrolled at the University of California, Los Angeles, where she studied literature and art, appearing in minor films with such actors as Mickey Rooney, Constance Bennett, June Allyson, Dick Powell and Claudette Colbert. Never nominated for an Oscar, she made her first and only appearance on March 29, 1951, when she presented the award for Best Sound Mixing to Thomas T. Moulton for Eve. Moulton for *Eve*. It was a nightmare evening, which she ended in tears when she discovered her torn dress. She auditioned for the TV adaptation of the *comic strip Li'l Abner,* but the project never materialized.

Consecration

In March 1952, Marilyn Monroe caused a scandal by posing nude for a calendar. This episode in her life, far from tarnishing her career, added to her notoriety (see Nudity in her career). She tells journalists that she posed to pay the rent. Later, when asked if she really had nothing on during the shoot, she quipped: *"No, I had the radio on", a* double entendre that could mean she had the radio on or was "dressed" with the radio on.

On April 7, 1952, she made the cover of *Life* magazine for the first time, described as *"The Talk of Hollywood"*. It was then that she began her romance with Joe DiMaggio, a living baseball legend who had just retired.

Film columnist Hedda Hopper described Marilyn as *"Saloon and Sex authority"*, while producer Jerry Wald said of her that she "walks like an antelope, at a standstill [she looks] like a *snake encoiling*, and when she speaks you don't hear her words, it's like she's whispering that she loves you".

She made four films in the following months. For RKO Pictures, she plays a supporting role in Fritz Lang's *The Devil Wakes at Night,* starring Barbara Stanwyck. Released in June 1952, the film was a critical and public success. She then took part in the comedy *Cinq mariages à l'essai* and the drama *Troublez-moi ce soir*, in which she played the lead role of a nanny who threatens to harm the child in her care. Critical acclaim was not forthcoming, and *Variety* described the film as "lightweight". In *Chérie, je me sens rajeunir*, in which she appears for the first time as a platinum blonde, she plays opposite Cary Grant and Ginger Rogers, under the direction of Howard Hawks. The film did well at the box office, despite some negative reviews.

Darryl F. Zanuck saw in her a strong commercial potential and hired her for 1953's *Niagara*, in which she performed her song *Kiss*, and played a femme fatale who wishes to have her husband, played by Joseph Cotten, murdered. Critics rave about the film, calling her performance "overtly sexual". Constance Bennett felt that Marilyn had "a great future ahead of her". Zanuck, however, had always despised her as an actress, and didn't hesitate to let her know it. The latter was followed by actress Joan Crawford, who described Marilyn, after her appearance at the Oscars, as "vulgar" and declared that her dress looked like a "potato sack".

The young woman becomes friends with Jane Russell on the set of Howard Hawks' *Les hommes préfèrent les blondes.* Russell, who described her partner as "very shy, very sweet and very intelligent", received US$400,000, while Marilyn was paid US$18,000 a week. In Los Angeles, when the film was released on June 26, 1953, both actresses left their footprints in the cement of Grauman's Chinese Theatre, right next to the *Hollywood Walk of Fame* on Hollywood Boulevard.

Her next film, Jean Negulesco's *How to Marry a Millionaire* (1953), starred Betty Grable and Lauren Bacall. Written by Nunnally Johnson, the story is about three female New York models who do everything in their power to marry millionaires. The films she made during this period helped boost her popularity. .

Marilyn Monroe talks to the *New York Times* about her desire to play dramatic roles. She expressed her desire to 20th Century Fox to be cast in the film *The Egyptian*. Darryl F. Zanuck objected without even giving her a screen test.

She signs on for *River of No Return*. She didn't get along with director Otto Preminger and refused to speak to him during filming. Robert Mitchum, her main partner, had to mediate. She later declares that she "deserved better than a cowboy Z-movie." At the end of 1953, Marilyn Monroe is scheduled to start shooting *The Girl in Pink Tights* with Frank Sinatra. When she refused, she was suspended by Fox.

On January 14, 1954, she married Joe DiMaggio and declared to the press: "My main ambition now is to devote myself to my marriage". The following month, while accompanying her husband to coach a baseball team in Japan, she was invited by the U.S. Army to spend four days in Korea, singing three songs from her recent films on nine occasions before a total of 60,000 American soldiers. This first stage experience enabled her to overcome her fear of crowds.

Back in Hollywood in March 1954, she settled her dispute with Fox and starred in *The Merry Parade*. Walter Lang's musical film was a flop. The film was also poorly received by critics, who described Marilyn Monroe's performance as "disastrous" and "embarrassing". The actress reveals that she only accepted the role on condition that she would then make *Seven Years of Thinking*. She began shooting the latter in September with Tom Ewell. It was in New York that she played the most famous scene of her entire career, the one in the subway grate where her white dress rises. Director Billy Wilder demanded many takes, which irritated Joe DiMaggio. After several arguments, Marilyn announced their separation. They divorced in November 1954 after eight months of marriage. She left Hollywood incognito on December 16, 1954, and moved to the New York home of her photographer and friend Milton Greene, with whom she founded *Marilyn Monroe Productions, Inc.* on December 31, 1954. Through this production company, she hoped to launch her new career in New York. Milton Greene, who felt that the major studios had offered her unworthy fees, convinced her to free herself from their tutelage. Having thus demonstrated her desire for independence, Marilyn was officially suspended by Fox on January 15, 1955.

In 1954, she also took singing lessons. RCA signed her to a contract, and her first record sold 75,000 copies.

In 1955, thanks to Truman Capote, she took acting lessons with British actress Constance Collier. Collier felt that Marilyn Monroe possessed a "beautiful, fragile and subtle talent". After a few weeks' work, the actress who had made her name in Alfred Hitchcock's *The Rope* died on May 21, 1955. At a meeting with Fox, Marilyn Monroe asked to work with Hitchcock. But the director retorted that he didn't like women with "sex on their faces". He preferred cool blondes like Grace Kelly or Tippi Hedren.

Actors Studio

While shooting *The Merry Parade*, Marilyn met Paula Strasberg and her daughter Susan. She asked them to study at the Actors Studio with Lee Strasberg. In March 1955, Monroe met Cheryl Crawford, co-founder of the Actors Studio, who introduced her to Lee Strasberg. After meeting her, he accepted her as a student.

In May, she begins dating the playwright Arthur Miller, whom she had met five years earlier. On June 1er , Marilyn's birthday, Joe DiMaggio accompanies her to the New York premiere of *Seven Years of Thinking* and throws a party in her honor. The evening ended with a public argument before Marilyn Monroe's hasty departure. They did not see each other for a long time' .

She continued to take classes at the Actors Studio and made friends with actors Kevin McCarthy and Eli Wallach, who described her as studious and sincere in her approach. She starred in the play *Anna Christie* with Maureen Stapleton, based on the work by Eugene O'Neill, without forgetting her lines during the performances, which had not been the case in rehearsals, where she failed every time. *Anna Christie's performance was* a great success, and the public applauded Marilyn. Although only a student, she is Lee Strasberg's proudest pupil ("I've worked with hundreds of actors and actresses, and there are only two who are much better than the rest. The first is Marlon Brando, and the second is Marilyn Monroe"), he took her under his protection (she found refuge in the Strasberg family home), and encouraged her to undergo psychoanalysis to get closer to the characters she was playing.

Meanwhile, *Seven Years of Thinking* becomes a huge success, grossing around US$8 million at the box office. Critics hail Marilyn Monroe's performance. Thanks to this success, she negotiates a new contract with 20th Century Fox that gives her more power: $100,000 per film, an extra $500 per week for miscellaneous expenses, a say in the script as well as in the director and cinematographer, and the right to act for studios other than Fox'.

The first film to be made under this new contract was Joshua Logan's *Bus Stop*, which approved of the star's working methods. Paula Strasberg became his personal advisor on all his films. Lee's wife wears on the nerves of directors Joshua Logan, Laurence Olivier, Billy Wilder, George Cukor and John Huston, all of whom have seen it all before. After each scene, Marilyn Monroe turns to her to see if her performance has lived up to her aspirations. A nod from Paula and Marilyn Monroe demands another take, even if the previous one seems perfect to everyone. Hated by all, Paula earns herself the nicknames "Black Mushroom" or "Witch" from the technicians, to whom she never speaks. Nevertheless, she reassures Marilyn Monroe, even though her presence is nonsense to many.

In *Arrêt d'autobus,* she played "Chérie", a cabaret singer who falls in love with a cowboy. Very pleased with her performance, Logan tried to get her nominated for a Best Actress Oscar. . She was nevertheless nominated for a Golden Globe.

She spent more time with Arthur Miller, with whom she had been having an affair for over a year. It was at this point that the press began to write about them, often dubbing them "*The egghead and the hourglass*". . They were married on June 29, 1956.

Arrêt d'autobus is followed by *Prince et la Danseuse,* also interpreted and directed by Laurence Olivier. Olivier hates Marilyn Monroe because of her whims on the set. Later, he described her as "marvelous, the best of all". The film was an abject failure. Nevertheless, she won critical acclaim, particularly in Europe, where in 1959 she won the Crystal Star and the David di Donatello for Best Foreign Actress, as well as a BAFA nomination for Best Foreign Actress.

Absent from the screen in 1958, she now lived with Arthur Miller on Long Island and miscarried on August 1er 1957' . He nevertheless encouraged her to return to Hollywood to star in *Certains l'aiment chaud*. The director knew, however, that she was often late, had stage fright, and had difficulty learning her lines when he directed her in *Sept ans de réflexion*. This time, Marilyn Monroe was hostile, refusing to shoot certain scenes' . Her incessant lateness undermined her friendship with Tony Curtis, who later declared that kissing her was "like kissing Hitler." The actor later said it was just a prank. Pregnant at the time of shooting, she miscarried again in December 1958, once the film had been completed.

Some Like It Hot was a resounding success and was nominated for five Oscars. Marilyn Monroe wins the Golden Globe for Best Actress in a Musical or Comedy for her performance. Billy Wilder declares the film their greatest success, although Marilyn always hated it. He also talks about the problems he encountered while making the film: "Marilyn was very difficult because she was totally unpredictable. I didn't know what day we were going to have [...] would she be cooperative or obstructive?" he says. However, he loves Marilyn Monroe and defines her as a comic actress of genius. He also mentioned other projects with her, including *Irma la Douce* with Shirley MacLaine.

Health problems

In the 1960s, her popularity was at its peak. She agreed to star in George Cukor's *The Billionaire.* Dissatisfied with the script, she had it rewritten by Arthur Miller. Gregory Peck was to play the male lead, but he eventually turned down the new script, as did Cary Grant, Charlton Heston, Yul Brynner and Rock Hudson, before it went to Yves Montand. Shooting was difficult for the actress, who didn't get along with the director. The openly homosexual director had a soft spot for the French actor, with whom Marilyn Monroe had an affair. This relationship ended when Montand refused to leave his wife Simone Signoret. The film was a critical and commercial failure.

It was at this time that her health problems began. She began consulting a Los Angeles psychiatrist, Dr. Ralph Greenson, whom she saw almost every day. Dr. Greenson exerted a decisive influence on his patient. According to him, her marriage had been strained for some time, despite Miller's best efforts to look after her. Greenson declared that his main objective at the time was to reduce Marilyn Monroe's drug intake.

She then starred in John Huston's *The Misfits.* The film, written for her by Arthur Miller, also stars Clark Gable, Montgomery Clift and Eli Wallach. Shooting began in July 1960. Often ill, Marilyn Monroe was unable to act. She was even hospitalized for ten days. Without Dr. Greenson's help, she returned to taking sleeping pills and alcohol. On November 16, 1960, Gable died of a heart attack in Los Angeles at the age of 59. Journalists blamed Marilyn Monroe's death on her frequent lateness on the set'. The film was not a commercial success, and reviews were mostly negative, although some praised the performances of Monroe and Gable.

Over the following months, she became increasingly dependent on alcohol and medication. She divorced Arthur Miller in January 1961, and drew up her will on January 14, 1961. She agreed to let her psychoanalyst Marianne Rie Kris commit her to the Payne Whitney (en) psychiatric clinic, where she was placed in a secure cell. She later described the experience as a "nightmare". Having the right to a phone call, she contacted Joe DiMaggio, who had her transferred to the open center at New York Presbyterian Hospital, where he remained close to her. After three weeks of treatment, she leaves the hospital, harassed by a crowd of reporters on her way out. Unable to perform, she returned to California to rest. Following this internment, she asked her lawyer Milton Rudin to change her will, but this was not done, and gave rise to controversy over the will on her death, notably over the "disabling influence" exerted by the Strasbergs and Marianne Rie Kris.

The year 1962

In the early 1960s, Marilyn Monroe was addicted to amphetamines, barbiturates and alcohol. She suffered from a variety of mental health problems, including depression, anxiety, low self-esteem and chronic insomnia.

The actress still owed Fox one last film, under the terms of her 1956 contract. The studio commissioned one of their screenwriters, Arnold Schulman, to remake a 1940 comedy, *My Favorite Wife,* starring Irene Dunne and Cary Grant. The story of a missing woman, presumed dead, who returns home to find her husband remarried. Frank Tashlin, director of Jerry Lewis comedies, is asked to direct the film. Marilyn Monroe, who wanted to return to the screen with an eventful film, initially refused the project, deeming it "insipid". With a say in the script and the director, she agreed to reconsider the project. Nunnally Johnson, who had worked with her on *How to Marry a Millionaire*, was then hired to sign a new version. George Cukor, who also owed Fox a film, initially turned down the project because of nightmarish memories of shooting The *Billionaire*. Threatened with legal action if he didn't honor his commitments, he resigned himself to accepting the studio's proposal (for US$300,000) and thus reuniting with Marilyn Monroe, whom he deeply despised. Despite an unfinished script, Marilyn Monroe signs on for *Something's Got to Give*. Under the terms of her non-exclusive contract with Fox, she still earned US$100,000 per film, seven times less than the Hollywood norm for a star of her standing.

At the age of thirty-five, she bought her first home with a mortgage, for US$35,000 in January 1962. It was Eunice Murray, her new housekeeper and former psychiatric nurse, who found her the modest neo-Mexican-inspired hacienda at 12305 Fifth Helena Drive, in Brentwood on the outskirts of Los Angeles.

On March 5, 1962, at the Golden Globes ceremony, the foreign press awarded her, for the second time, the "World's Leading Actress for 1961" prize. Accompanied by screenwriter José Bolanos, she was drunk and received the award from Rock Hudson, staggering and stammering out a few thank-yous in front of the stunned audience. In order not to embarrass her, the ceremony was not broadcast.

Meanwhile, Nunnally Johnson delivers the finished script for *Something's Got to Give*, which Marilyn Monroe approves. Dissatisfied, George Cukor hires his friend Walter Bernstein to rewrite the dialogue, which he deems "too bland". His partners Dean Martin and Cyd Charisse were also hired. On the eve of shooting, scheduled to start on April 23, Marilyn Monroe comes down with a fever and informs the studio that she will be absent. Cukor begins shooting all the scenes in which she is not present. Marilyn consults her doctor, Dr. Engelberg, on the same day. He diagnosed chronic sinusitis, and Lee Siegel, the studio's official physician, recommended postponing shooting for a month, which the studio refused. On April 30, Marilyn Monroe went to the set for the first time and shot 90 minutes of rushes against Dr. Siegel's advice. She fell ill and was evacuated from the studio. She was reunited with the crew and shot scenes around a swimming pool for three days in early May.

Taking advantage of a lunch break, she once again left the set - despite a studio ban - to attend John Fitzgerald Kennedy's birthday party in New York, during which she sang the famous *Happy Birthday, Mister President* . Jackie Kennedy objected to her attendance at her husband's private party, preferring to retire to Virginia with her children.

The actress returned to Hollywood to shoot her scenes, which "enchanted" the Fox bosses. Despite several days of trouble-free shooting, she showed signs of nervousness and was unable to learn her lines, which irritated Cukor, who eventually lost his temper with her. On June 1[er] , her 36th birthday[e] , she returned to the set, where a party was organized at the end of the day in her honor: it was her last professional appearance. On the 7th, Fox leaks to the press that Marilyn Monroe has been fired and that "Kim Novak and every other actress in Hollywood and beyond" has been contacted to replace her. The studio sues Marilyn Monroe for US$500,000. Peter Levathes, head of production at Fox, tells the star: "The star system has lost all control. We let the lunatics run the asylum and they practically destroyed it."

However, Kim Novak, Shirley MacLaine and others (including Brigitte Bardot) decline the offer to reprise her role. The studio officially announces that Lee Remick has finally been chosen. Dean Martin objected, refusing to resume filming without Marilyn. Fox sued him and also claimed US$500,000 for breach of contract. The film crew was soon suspended. Cyd Charisse in turn sued Dean Martin, claiming US$14,000 in damages for loss of earnings. For their part, Fox increased the charges in their lawsuit against Marilyn Monroe, claiming US$750,000. On June 19, the studio again turned against Dean Martin, with Fox's lawyers demanding US$3,339,000. The actor counters and sues Fox for US$6,885,000 in damages. The case hit the headlines, with some headlines even repeating the actor's words: *"No Marilyn, no picture!* A year later, the lawsuit was dropped.

Negotiations began immediately, and on June 20, Fox announced that filming would resume shortly. Marilyn Monroe, as part of a public relations campaign to restore her public image, participates in photo shoots with several leading photographers and interviews with major magazines. She and DiMaggio talk of remarrying, and a date is even set: August 8, 1962. Other film projects discussed included *I Love Louisa* and *The Jean Harlow Story*. Her dispute with Fox was resolved and her contract renewed. *Something's Got to Give was* due to resume production in early autumn. Peter Levathes went to her home for a conciliation meeting. At the end of the meeting, Marilyn Monroe was assured a new script, the lawsuits against her were dropped, George Cukor was officially fired and replaced by Jean Negulesco, who had directed *How to Marry a Millionaire*, and a new million-dollar contract was signed for two films: US$250,000 to complete *Something's Got to Give* and US$750,000 for another film to be determined' . Marilyn Monroe, who had appeared in thirty films, was now thirty-six.

In June 1962, Marilyn took part in a final photo shoot, later named *The Last Sitting*.

At the end of July, depressed, she confided to her hairdresser that she had just had an abortion [ref. to be confirmed]. At least two doctors wrote her numerous prescriptions for sleeping pills in the last week of her life.

Friday August 3 was devoted to numerous business and private telephone calls, and meetings with her psychiatrist and her friend Pat Newcomb. Saturday was the same: phone calls, work in the garden with Dr. Greenson and a walk on the beach with actor Peter Lawford, the Kennedys' brother-in-law. Some accounts describe her under the influence of tranquilizers. At 7:45 p.m., she has another telephone conversation with Lawford, in which she sounds depressed and confused. He calls back a little later, but the line is out of order. He makes several calls to relatives in an attempt to reach her. Finally reached, Eunice Murray, the housekeeper hired at Dr. Greenson's request, reports that all is well: it's 8:30 p.m. at this point. According to Donald Spoto, author of a biography of Marilyn Monroe, she was already dead or dying of overdose.

Death

Marilyn Monroe died on the night of August 4-5, 1962. Nearly five hours elapsed between the estimated time of death, around 9:30 and 10 p.m., and the phone call to the police from the Greensons, along with Mrs. Murray and Dr. Engelberg. After investigation, the Los Angeles coroner noted on his file: "Suicide probable". His death was never solved, and from 1962 onwards, the FBI and CIA were accused of homicide.

In Los Angeles, rumors have it that on the day of Marilyn Monroe's death, Bobby Kennedy and his brother-in-law Peter Lawford came to see Marilyn Monroe twice; Bobby told her that neither he nor John would accept her calls, as he and John F. Kennedy wanted to put an end to rumors about their relationship. A heated argument ensued. Lacking evidence, the testimonies have never been corroborated and remain nothing more than speculation.

According to the actress's phone records, at 8:30 p.m. she received a call from Peter Lawford inviting her to dinner, but she declined. He said she looked *groggy*. Her last call was at 10 pm. She called her photographer, Ralph Robert. But he didn't answer. According to the operator who took the call, Marilyn was barely able to speak. While she thought Marilyn had fallen asleep on the phone, the coroner declared that it was around this time that Marilyn died. Worried that Marilyn had locked the door, something she never did, her housekeeper Eunice Murray called psychiatrist Ralph Greenson and Dr. Hengelberg. Arriving on the scene, Greenson broke her bedroom window and said, verbatim: "I think we've lost her. Long hours passed before they called the police and ambulance, claiming that in shock, they preferred to break the news to the studios first. Sergeant Jack Clemmons said that Doctors Greenson and Hengelberg seemed distant, and noted the curious attitude of the housekeeper as she put the laundry through the washing machine. Also, he found Marilyn's position suspicious; she was in what he called the "gendarme position", with her arms at her sides, whereas usually a person dying of an overdose is often curled up in pain. Based on an overdose of sleeping pills in her body, the judge's verdict on Marilyn Monroe's death was "probable suicide", leaving all kinds of allegations open.

At the morgue, Marilyn's usual hairdresser Agnès Flanagan (Jean Harlow's hairdresser, whom she had hired to do her famous platinum-blonde coloring) is unable to dress Marilyn's hair, too damaged by years of treatment (peroxide for coloring, caustic soda for straightening) but also by the autopsy. A wig is put on, copying the hairstyle she wore in her last film *Something's Got to Give* and sparking rumors that she was already wearing a wig during filming, as well as for the earlier *Les Désaxés*.

Marilyn was buried on August 8, 1962 at the *Westwood Village Memorial Park Cemetery* in Los Angeles. Her half-sister, Berniece Miracle, with the help of Joe DiMaggio, organized the private funeral, which, despite protests, was not attended by her star friends Dean Martin and Frank Sinatra. However, hundreds of onlookers lined the streets around the cemetery. Distraught, her ex-husband bent over her coffin and whispered "I love you" three times. The ceremony ends with one of Marilyn's favorite songs, Judy Garland's *Over the Rainbow.* She is then laid to rest in Grave 24 of the *Corridor of Memories*.

Marilyn was an international star, and her sudden death made headlines in the U.S. and Europe. According to Lois Banner, the suicide rate in Los Angeles doubled the month after her death; the circulation of most newspapers increased that month, and the *Chicago Tribune* reported that it had received hundreds of phone calls from people asking for information about her death. Jean Cocteau declared that his death should be a terrible lesson for all those whose job consists mainly of spying on and tormenting movie stars. Her former co-star Laurence Olivier called her "a complete victim of Ballyhoo and sensation", and Joshua Logan (director of *Bus Stop*), said she was one of the world's most unsung people.

On August 17, 1962, *Life* magazine reissued her last interview, "*A Last Long Talk With A Lonely Girl*" by Richard Meryman, previously published on August 3, 1962, two days before her death.

Uncertainties surrounding the cause of death

On August 5, 1962, at around 3 a.m., Eunice Murray, Marilyn Monroe's housekeeper, was worried that the actress had locked herself in her room, leaving the light on but not answering her call. She alerts psychiatrist Ralph Greenson, who arrives on the scene, breaks the glass of the bedroom window and discovers the actress dead on her bed, one hand on the telephone receiver, the bedside table littered with boxes of pills and an empty bottle of Nembutal on the floor. Greenson called Hyman Engelberg, Marilyn's personal physician, who arrived at her home around 3:50 a.m. and officially declared her dead. Sergeant Jack Clemmons of the West Los Angeles Police Department receives a phone call at 4:25 a.m. from Hyman Engelberg, who informs him of the actress's suicide. Clemmons was the first police officer to arrive at the star's Brentwood home.

The report by medical examiner Thomas Noguchi speaks of a "probable suicide" due to an accidental overdose of barbiturates (*acute barbiturate poisoning ingestion of overdose*) .

Faced with a summary autopsy report and the disappearance of the liver, kidneys and stomach, the district attorney, John Miner (en), was the first to consider the hypothesis of assassination.

Due to a lack of evidence, investigators have neither closed the case, nor said whether it was suicide or homicide. According to some rumors, Marilyn Monroe was the victim of a plot hatched by the FBI and CIA to accumulate evidence against the Kennedys. These rumors were taken up by novelist Norman Mailer in his book *Marilyn - A Biography* (1974), which legitimized the assassination, although he later admitted that it was pure fiction made for profit.

Don Wolfe, in his books *The Last Days of Marilyn Monroe* (1998) and *The Assassination of Marilyn Monroe* (1999), supports the hypothesis of a state assassination. This version would involve Robert Kennedy and a whole group of people close to the actress, who would have kept silent for years.

According to Donald Spoto, Marilyn died as the result of a medical error. She was given a chloral hydrate enema, prepared by her psychoanalyst Ralph Greenson (chloral helped her sleep), after having taken Nembutal, a potentially fatal mixture.

In 1985, when the case of Marilyn Monroe's death was reopened in Los Angeles, Grand Jury President Sam Cordova opposed District Attorney Ira Reiner, requesting additional investigations to clarify unanswered questions. The request for an investigation into Robert Kennedy's involvement is rejected on the basis of evidence.

In 2005, the *Los Angeles Times* published extracts from Marilyn's interviews with her psychiatrist, as reported by an investigator into her death, in which the star allegedly questioned her career, her looks, her marriages, and revealed that she had had an affair with Joan Crawford. After her death, the prosecutor in charge of the investigation, John Miner, is said to have obtained from the star's psychiatrist, Dʳ Ralph Greenson, the recordings of Marilyn's sessions on his couch, and to have taken extensive notes. In these notes, Marilyn Monroe is said to have become obsessed with the Oscars and to have wondered about her career, including the idea of playing William Shakespeare to finally be considered a serious actress. She also reportedly told her psychiatrist how she examined herself in the mirror, naked, to observe the effect of age on her body, finding that "my breasts are starting to sag a little, (but) my waist is still fine, and my buttocks are still the best." She would also talk about Clark Gable, in whom she would seek fatherly love, and her marriages and divorces with baseball player Joe DiMaggio and playwright Arthur Miller. Finally, she would reveal that she had a one-night lesbian affair with actress Joan Crawford. "The next time I saw Crawford, she wanted to do it again, but I told her frankly that I didn't really enjoy doing it with a woman. After that, she blamed me." The psychiatrist allegedly allowed John Miner to listen to the tapes on condition that he never revealed their contents. Miner only broke this promise of secrecy years after the psychiatrist's death, when some of the actress's biographers suggested that he might be considered a suspect in the star's death.

According to the prosecutor, listening to the tapes, it would be obvious "that it was absolutely impossible for this woman to have committed suicide. She had definite plans for her future, she knew exactly what she wanted to do. Lee Strasberg told her she has to play Shakespeare, and she's fascinated by the idea." The prosecutor believes that the actress was murdered: after putting her to sleep with something in her drink, she was given Nembutal dissolved in water, in high doses, in the form of an enema. However, Prosecutor Miner's claims are questioned by many biographers, and contradicted by several witnesses, including the former deputy prosecutor and the widow of psychiatrist Ralph Greenson, who told the *Los Angeles Times* that her husband had never mentioned the existence of the tapes'. Only John Miner's transcriptions exist, according to which Dr Ralph Greenson destroyed the tapes.

While the theory of state-sponsored assassination seems to have been definitively ruled out, there remain only those of suicide or accident. The suicide theory rests on fragile foundations (sudden melancholic decompensation linked to his bipolar disorders); then there remains that of an accident due to the mixing of barbiturates with alcohol, which would have led to cardiac distress, or of an accident caused by his psychiatrist's enema, the case remains open' .

Marilyn Monroe suffered from endometriosis, forcing her to ingest large doses of medication to cope with the pain. During her operation by Leon Krohn and Marcus Rabwin, an advanced stage of endometriosis was discovered in April 1952, instead of appendicitis, for which she underwent surgery. She underwent seven operations between 1952 and 1962. Two of her biographers, Anthony Summers (1985) and Donald Spoto (1993), discuss the gynecological suffering to which the actress had been subjected since her adolescence, sometimes forcing her to stop driving suddenly and bend over in pain on the side of the road. Numerous boxes of painkillers prescribed for menstrual pain were also seen on the actress's dressing table. According to Martin Winckler, Marilyn Monroe's death was caused by the massive ingestion of endometriosis painkillers.

Posterity

Popularity

Almost sixty years after her death, Marilyn Monroe remains one of the world's best-known actresses. Numerous documentaries and biographies have been devoted to her, and several TV films have retraced her life, starring actresses such as Ashley Judd and Poppy Montgomery. She was recently played by Charlotte Sullivan in the mini-series *The Kennedys* and Michelle Williams in *My Week with Marilyn*. In 2022, the 60th anniversary of Marilyn's death, the biopic Blonde, based on the book by Joyce Carol Oates, will be released on Netflix, starring Ana de Armas as Marilyn Monroe.

Her image is still widely used on magazine covers, in advertisements, for derivative products such as make-up, and in films, such as *Pulp Fiction*, *L.A. Confidential* and *The Simpsons,* where the subway scene from *Seven Years' Thinking can be* seen. In 2006, Nicole Kidman lent her voice to the character of *Norma Jean* in the cartoon *Happy Feet*. She is also featured in a number of songs, including *Candle in the Wind* , *Goodbye Yellow Brick Road* by Elton John, *Vogue* and *Material Girl* by Madonna, Norma Jean Baker written and composed by Serge Gainsbourg and sung by Jane Birkin, Marilyn & John sung by Vanessa Paradis, Black Marilyn by Shy'm and *Marilyn Monroe* by Pharrell Williams.

In 2012, Marilyn Monroe still generated an annual income estimated by Forbes magazine at $27 million. She is therefore considered the world's most lucrative female icon.

For the anecdote, the five hundred and seventy-six lots auctioned by Christie's on Wednesday and Thursday, October 27 and 28, 1999 in New York had been bequeathed by Marilyn to Lee Strasberg with the idea that he would pass them on to their circle of friends, which he didn't do: the goods were hoarded and, on Lee's death, passed on to his second wife, Anna Strasberg, who finally decided to sell them. The total auction price, estimated at between ten and fifteen million dollars, came to $13.4 million. At the time of his death, his bank account showed a balance of $800,000 ($7,744,000 today).

The actress was also the subject of a famous series of silkscreen prints by the "pope" of Pop art, Andy Warhol, which began in 1964 with "*Shot Sage Blue Marilyn*". It is one of the artist's most widely reproduced works to date. In 1967, the *Hommage to Marilyn Monroe* exhibition at New York's Sydney Janis Gallery brought together many artists of the "Pop" trend.

Marilyn Monroe's dresses

The white dress from *Sept ans de réflexion*

Marilyn Monroe is regarded as a cultural icon in the history of cinema, notably with the image taken from a scene in Billy Wilder's film *The Seven Year Itch* (1955), in which the actress, wearing a white dress, stands over a subway grate whose draught lifts her dress.

In September 1954, she began shooting *Seven Years of Thinking*, playing the lead role in "The Girl", a woman who becomes the object of her married neighbor's sexual fantasies. Although the film was shot in Hollywood, the studio decided to promote it early by shooting a scene in Manhattan on Lexington Avenue. The scene lasts several hours, and attracts a crowd of almost 2,000 spectators, including professional photographers. The white dress appears in the sequence where Marilyn Monroe and co-star Tom Ewell leave the Trans-Lux Theater on 52nd Street. When they hear a subway train pass under the sidewalk grate, Monroe's character steps up to the grate, saying "Ooh, do you feel the subway breeze?" as the wind lifts the dress and exposes her legs.

After the actress's death in 1962, costume designer
Travilla kept the dress under lock and key, along with
many other costumes he had made for Marilyn over the
years, so much so that it was dubbed a "lost collection". It
was only after her death in 1990 that Travilla's colleague
Bill Sarris exhibited the garments. The dress later joined
actress Debbie Reynolds' private collection of Hollywood
memorabilia at the Hollywood Motion Picture Museum.
During an interview with Oprah Winfrey, talking about
Monroe's dress, Debbie Reynolds declared that the dress
had become ecru "because, as you know, it's very very old
now". In 2011, however, she announced that she would
sell her collection in a phased auction, the first of which
would take place on June 18, 2011. Prior to the auction, it
was estimated that Marilyn's dress would sell for between
one and two million dollars, but it actually sold for over
$5.6 million ($4.6 million, plus a commission of one
million) .

JFK's birthday dress

In May 2022, at the Metropolitan Museum of Art gala in
New York, businesswoman Kim Kardashian wore the dress
that dressed Marilyn Monroe at President John F.
Kennedy's birthday party on May 19, 1962. The flesh-
toned dress, designed by Bob Mackie and hand-
embroidered with 2,500 crystals, was bought at auction in
2016 by *Ripley's Believe It or Not!*, "a media empire that

also owns a chain of museums" for a record $4.8 million. It was first purchased at auction by businessman Martin Zweig for $1.3 million. Bob Mackie's drawing of the dress sold for $10,000.

Heritage

Marilyn Monroe, grateful to Anna Freud who received and listened to her while she was filming *The Prince and the Dancer* in London, included the Anna Freud Centre in her will, bequeathing "25% of her fortune and future royalties". This bequest continues to generate income for the foundation, with business around the actress generating "around 10 million euros a year thanks to the many brands that still use her image"[ref. needed]. By the age of 21, Marilyn had read Sigmund Freud's *The Interpretation of Dreams*, and had also come close to starring in a film directed by Jean-Paul Sartre, who wanted Marilyn Monroe to play the role. "But *Freud, secret passions* was ultimately made without him and without the actress.

Privacy policy

Weddings

Marilyn Monroe was married three times:

- from June 19, 1942 to September 13, 1946 with James Dougherty ;

- January 14 to October 27, 1954 with Joe DiMaggio;

- from June 29, 1956 to January 24, 1961 with Arthur Miller.

In 1942, at the age of sixteen, she married James Dougherty, nicknamed "Lucky Jim" for marrying her. She nicknamed him "Daddy" and called herself "Baby". As a child, Marilyn Monroe lacked everything, and when James enlisted in the Navy, she fell apart and felt abandoned once again. She later declared that "the marriage had been neither happy nor unhappy." For her, this first separation was a mere formality.

Of Sicilian origin, baseball champion Joe DiMaggio, the most famous of the 1950s, fell under her spell, divorced her and married her in 1954. Their story enthralled the whole of America. But DiMaggio's love for her work and her public caused the couple to fall apart nine months later. Although they still love each other, the court officially accuses her of mental cruelty.

To love, Marilyn Monroe also needed to admire. Such was the case with writer Arthur Miller, who was fascinated by her. After their marriage in 1956, Miller changed his mind and was quick to say the most horrifying things about her: "She's a mean, narcissistic monster who took my energy and drained me of my talent." Marilyn Monroe thought she had found happiness and balance with him, but despite all her efforts, including her conversion to Judaism″ , the couple separated in 1961.

Other relationships

On the set of Le *Milliardaire,* Marilyn Monroe fell under the spell of her partner Yves Montand. Montand's partner Simone Signoret declares: "If Marilyn is in love with my husband, it's proof that she has good taste. Montand eventually tired of the actress's sincere feelings for him, and returned to Signoret. In 2017, Frieda Hull, a photographer and friend of the late star, claimed that Marilyn had become pregnant with Yves Montand's child in 1960. The actress reportedly asked Frieda to keep it a secret. However, the pregnancy ended in another miscarriage.

For a long time, Clark Gable symbolized the ideal man for Marilyn Monroe, who liked to imagine that her father resembled him. During the filming of Les *Désaxés,* Gable courteously ignored the fact that the actress was in love with him.

Shortly before his death, Cass Chaplin, the youngest son of actor Charlie Chaplin, wrote in his memoirs that he had had a friendly, then amorous relationship with the actress, a fact that biographer Anthony Summers also noted in his book about the star. There is no precise chronology for this relationship. However, Summers asserts that Cass Chaplin even made the relationship official with her parents for Christmas in 1947. The affair ended when Cass Chaplin discovered that Marilyn Monroe was cheating on him with his best friend, Eddie G. Robbinson Jr, son of a prominent film producer of the time.

Relations with the Kennedys

On May 19, 1962, Marilyn Monroe made her last major public appearance, almost drunk, singing *Happy Birthday, Mr. President on the* occasion of President John Fitzgerald Kennedy's birthday at Madison Square Garden. The ultra-sheer dress she wore on this occasion sold at auction in 1999 for $1.3 million. This sheath dress, in pink silk gauze studded with 2,500 rhinestones, became the world's most expensive gown, beating out the one Princess Diana wore to dance with John Travolta, which sold for $222,500 in June 1997.

As early as the 1960s, rumors circulated about the star's relationship with John Fitzgerald Kennedy and his brother Robert Kennedy.

The relationship was not confirmed until 1970, when Frank Cappell published *The Strange Death of Marilyn Monroe*. Another of JFK's lovers, Judith Campbell, also wrote about it in her autobiography, published in 1977.

Marilyn Monroe and religion

Marilyn Monroe's Jewish prayer book (Siddur) is up for auction in New York in October 2018. She would have received it after her marriage to Arthur Miller and her conversion to Judaism. The Siddur is inscribed in English with *Daily Prayers* and is said to have a connection with the "Avenue N Jewish Center" in Brooklyn, New York, which Arthur Miller frequented. They were civilly married on June 29, 1956, at the *Westchester County* Courthouse, and two days later, on July 1er 1956, they had a religious ceremony, and Rabbi Robert Goldburg converted Marilyn Monroe to Judaism.

Rabbi Goldberg published on this subject in 2010, in *Reform Judaism magazine*. Even after her divorce from Arthur Miller on January 24, 1961, Marilyn Monroe continued to consider herself Jewish, admiring the ethical values of Judaism. Until her death a year later, she kept her Siddur and a Menorah, which played the Hatikvah, the Israeli national anthem.

Filmography

- 1947: *Dangerous Years* by Arthur Pierson: Evie

- 1948: *Choisie entre toutes* (*You Were Meant for Me*) by Lloyd Bacon: a young girl (uncredited) (unconfirmed)

- 1948: *Bagarre pour une blonde* (*Scudda Hoo! Scudda Hay!*) by Hugh Herbert: Betty (uncredited)

- 1948: Louis King's *Green Grass of Wyoming*: a square-dancer (uncredited)

- 1948: *Ladies of the Chorus* by Phil Karlson: Peggy Martin

- 1949: David Miller's *Love Happy*: Grunion's client

- 1950: *Le Petit Train du Far West* (*A Ticket to Tomahawk*) by Richard Sale: Clara (uncredited)

- 1950: *Torment* (*Right Cross*) by John Sturges: Dusky Ledoux (uncredited)

- 1950: *The Fireball* by Tay Garnett: Polly

- 1950: The *Asphalt Jungle* by John Huston: Angela Phinlay

- 1950: *Eve* (*All About Eve*) by Joseph L. Mankiewicz: Claudia Caswell

- 1951: *Chéri, divorçons* (*Let's Make It Legal*) by Richard Sale: Joyce Mannering

- 1951: *Home Town Story* by Arthur Pierson: Iris Martin

- 1951: *Rendez-moi ma femme* (*As Young as You Feel*) by Harmon Jones: Harriet

- 1951: *Love Nest* by Joseph M. Newman: Roberta "Bobbie" Stevens

- 1952: *La Sarabande des pantins* (*O. Henry's Full House*), segment *The Cop and the Anthem* by Henry Koster: the prostitute

- 1952: *Monkey Business* by Howard Hawks: Lois Laurel

- 1952: *Clash by Night* by Fritz Lang: Peggy

- 1952: *Cinq Mariages à l'essai* (*We're Not Married!*) by Edmund Goulding: Anabel Norris

- 1952: *Troublez-moi ce soir* (*Don't Bother to Knock*) by Roy Ward Baker: Nell Forbes

- 1953: *Niagara* by Henry Hathaway: Rose Loomis

- 1953: Howard Hawks' *Gentlemen Prefer Blondes*: Lorelei Lee

- 1953: *Comment épouser un millionnaire* (*How to Marry a Millionaire*) by Jean Negulesco: Pola Debevoise

- 1954: River *of No Return* by Otto Preminger: Kay Weston

- 1954: Walter Lang's *La Joyeuse Parade* (*There's No Business Like Show Business)*: Vicky

- 1955: Billy Wilder's *The Seven Year* Itch: The Daughter

- 1956: *Bus Stop* by Joshua Logan: Cherie

- 1957: *The Prince and the Showgirl* by Laurence Olivier: Elsie Marina

- 1959: Billy Wilder's *Some Like It Hot*: Sugar Kane Kowalczyk

- 1960: *The Billionaire* (*Let's Make Love*) by George Cukor: Amanda Dell

- 1961: *The Misfits* by John Huston: Roslyn Taber

- 1962: George Cukor's *Marilyn Monroe: The Last Days* (*Something's Got to Give*) (unfinished): Ellen Wagstaff Arden

Claire Guibert lent her voice to Marilyn in most of the French versions of her films; the actress was also dubbed by Mony Dalmès for *Les hommes préfèrent les blondes* and *Comment épouser un millionnaire*.

Songs

To this list can be added the famous *live* rendition of *Happy Birthday, Mr. President* for John Fitzgerald Kennedy's birthday.

Publications

- Marilyn Monroe (trans. Tiphaine Samoyault), *Fragments. Poèmes, écrits intimes, lettres*, Paris, Le Seuil, 2010, 264 p. (ISBN 978-2-02-102328-2)

- Marilyn Monroe and Ben Hecht (transl. from English), *Confession inachevée*, Paris, Robert Laffont, 2011, 240 p. (ISBN 978-2-221-12743-8)

Awards

- On June 26, 1953, Marilyn Monroe and Jane Russell "immortalized" their hand and footprints in the courtyard of Grauman's Chinese Theatre.

- The actress also received her Hollywood star on the Hollywood Walk of Fame, at 6774 Hollywood Boulevard, following a ceremony held on February 8, 1960.

Awards

- Photoplay 1952: special magazine award

- Photoplay 1953: magazine's most popular female star

- Golden Globes 1954: Henrietta Award

- 1958 David di Donatello: best foreign actress for *The Prince and the Dancer*

- 1959 Crystal Stars: Best Foreign Actress for *The Prince and the Dancer*

- Golden Globes 1960: Best Actress for *Some Like It Hot*

- Golden Globes 1962: Henrietta Award

Appointments

- British Academy Film Awards 1956: Best Actress for *Seven Years of Reflection*

- Golden Globes 1956: Best Actress for *Bus Stop*

- British Academy Film Awards 1958: Best Actress for *The Prince and the Dancer*

Posthumous tributes

- In 1999, the American Film Institute ranked her sixth among the greatest American actresses of all time in *AFI's 100 Years... 100 Stars*" .

- In 2009, Marilyn Monroe was ranked no.° 1 in *Film's Sexiest Women of All Time* on the *TV Guide Network*.

- Asteroid (3768) Monroe was named in his honor.

- *Forever Marilyn* is a giant statue of Marilyn Monroe designed by Seward Johnson. The statue is a representation of one of Monroe's most famous images, taken from Billy Wilder's film *The Seven Year Itch*. Created in 2011, it has been exhibited at various locations in the United States, as well as in Australia. It has provoked controversy and been vandalized with red paint.

- Wax statues at Madame Tussauds museums on Hollywood Boulevard at the museum entrance. A statue at 3377 S Las Vegas Blvd #2001, Las Vegas, NV 89109, USA, 234 W 42nd St, New York NY 10036, USA, a statue of Marilyn at 1001 F St NW, Washington, DC 20004, USA, Dam 20, 1012 NP Amsterdam Netherlands, a statue of Marilyn at

Unter den Linden 74, 10117 Berlin, Germany, a statue of Marilyn at 87-89 Promenade, Blackpool FY1 5AA, United Kingdom, Marilyn statue at Marylebone Rd, London NW1 5LR, United Kingdom, Marilyn statue at Riesenradplatz, 1022 Wien, Austria, Marilyn statue at 6th Floor, Siam Discovery, 989 Rama I Road, Bangkok 10330, Thailand, Marilyn statue at Shop P101, The Peak Tower, No. 128 Peak Road, The Peak, Hong Kong, the Marilyn statue at Odaiba 1-6-1 Decks Tokyo Beach Island Mall 3FMinato-ku, Tokyo, 135-0091, Japan, the Marilyn statue at 10/F, New World Building, No.2-68 Nanjing Xi Road, Shanghai , China, a statue of Marilyn at Madame Tussauds Wuhan 21 Han Street 430000, Wuhan, China, a statue of Marilyn at Aquarium Wharf, Darling Harbour/Wheat Rd, Sydney NSW 2000, Australia.

- A statue of Marilyn in the town where her paternal grandfather was born. From the family genealogy of Marilyn's father (assuming he was indeed her father), we know that her paternal grandfather, Martin Mortensen, was born in Haugesund, a port town on the west coast of Norway between Stavanger and Bergen. Marilyn's father, Martin Edward Mortensen, may also have lived there, although he was born in California. A statue in tribute to the star and her roots stands along the harbor.

Works inspired by the artist

Statues

Monroe was the subject of a statue in Holywood, entitled *Forever Marilyn*, which provoked much controversy for its provocative nature, so much so that it was even vandalized with red paint. The statue is a representation of one of Monroe's most famous images, taken from Billy Wilder's film *The Seven Year Itch.*

Graphic arts

Marilyn Monroe has been represented by many painters and pop artists, including :

Theater

- 1964: *After the* Fall, play in two acts by Arthur Miller, directed by Elia Kazan, starring Barbara Loden

- 2004: *Finishing the Picture*, play in two acts by Arthur Miller, directed by Robert Falls, with Frances Fisher

- 2011: *Norma Jeane*, a two-act play by John Arnold loosely based on the novel by Joyce Carol Oates, directed by the author, with Marion Malenfant

- 2011: *Norma Jeane*, play by Pierre Glénat

- 2014: *Fragments* by and directed by Samuel Doux based on the actress's correspondence, with Lolita Chammah

- 2015 : *Bombshell*, a musical by Marc Shaiman and Scott Wittman based on the TV series *Smash*, starring Megan Hilty.

- 2022 : *Le Vertige Marilyn* by Olivier Steiner, directed by Olivier Steiner and Emmanuel Lagarrigue, starring Isabelle Adjani.

- 2023: *Bungalow 21* by Éric-Emmanuel Schmitt, directed by Jérome Lippman and starring Emmanuelle Seigner.

By herself

- 2010: *Fragments*, correspondence - letters and poems

- 2011: *Unfinished confession*, autobiography

By other authors

- 1962: *Marilyn et moi* by Susan Strasberg, autobiographical novel

- 1966: *The Prince, the Showgirl, and Me: Six Months on the Set with Marilyn and Olivier* by Colin Clark, autobiographical novel

- 2000: *Blonde* by Joyce Carol Oates, fictionalized biography

- 2006: *Marilyn, dernières séances de* Michel Schneider', **novel - Winner of the Prix Interallié**

- 2006: *Norma, novel*, by Daniel Charneux, novel - Winner of the Prix Charles Plisnier

- 2012: *Une semaine avec Marilyn* by Colin Clark, autobiographical novel

- 2015 : *La Drôle de vie de Zelda Zonk* by Laurence Peyrin, novel - Winner of the Prix Maison de la Presse

- 2022 : *Musée Marilyn* by Anne Savelli, , éditions Inculte, 2022.

Graphic novel

- *Holy Wood - Portrait fantasmé de Marilyn Monroe*, script and drawing by Tommy Redolfi, 256 pages, La Boîte à bulles, 2016.

Other books by United Library

https://campsite.bio/unitedlibrary

www.ingramcontent.com/pod-product-compliance
Lightning Source LLC
LaVergne TN
LVHW012153020425
807628LV00009B/238